The Book of Luke

The Book of Luke

TED BROSS

gatekeeper press
Columbus, Ohio

This book is a work of fiction. The names, characters and events in this book are the products of the author's imagination or are used fictitiously. Any similarity to real persons living or dead is coincidental and not intended by the author.

The Book of Luke: 9 Years in a Young Boy's Life

Published by Gatekeeper Press

2167 Stringtown Rd, Suite 109

Columbus, OH 43123-2989

www.GatekeeperPress.com

Copyright © 2018 by Ted Bross

All rights reserved. Neither this book, nor any parts within it may be sold or reproduced in any form or by any electronic or mechanical means, including information storage and retrieval systems without permission in writing from the author. The only exception is by a reviewer, who may quote short excerpts in a review.

ISBN: 9781642371062

eISBN: 9781642371079

Printed in the United States of America

Contents

Chapter 1-Age 4: Cousins 1
Chapter 2-Age 5: The Uniform 3
Chapter 3-Age 6: Bangers and Mash 5
Chapter 4-Age 7: The New Coach 11
Chapter 5-Age 8: The Injury 17
Chapter 6-Age 9: The Move 23
Chapter 7-Age 10: The Travel Team 27
Chapter 8-Age 11: The Decision 31
Chapter 9-Age 12: Middle School, Girls and the Rest of Life. 37
About The Author 41

Dedicated to my current grandchildren and future grandchildren yet to come

An hour with your grandchildren can make you feel young again. Anything longer than that, and you start to age quickly.

.

—ANONYMOUS

CHAPTER 1
Age 4: Cousins

It was still very dark but Luke's eyes were wide open as he looked around his room. He knew it was his birthday and couldn't wait any more. His cousin, Eli, was coming. Luke liked Eli very much. They were about the same age and looked like brothers. Eli was a little older and a little taller but when they were together, people thought they were twins.

Finally, the sun came through the window and Luke rushed down the stairs. Eli wasn't coming for a few more hours, but Luke still couldn't help but open the front door, just to make sure Eli wasn't there. At breakfast, mom and dad and baby brother Jack all wished Luke a happy birthday. This made Luke feel so grown up, now that he was finally four years old.

Later that morning, a shiny white car drove into Luke's driveway. He could see the back window open and there was Eli, yelling "Happy Birthday Luke," as the car came to a stop. Eli jumped out of the car and ran to give Luke a giant hug.

He loved Eli and Eli loved him. Eli ran back to his car and pulled out a big box, wrapped in red paper topped with a giant white ribbon. "This is for you Luke," said Eli. "I know we're supposed to wait to give you your present but I wanted to give it to you now."

Luke took the box and began to unwrap the paper as fast as he could. His mom and dad came out of the house and Luke stopped for a minute. "Is it ok to open this now?" he asked. "Of course it is," his mom answered. Luke tore off the rest of the paper and looked at the box. It was a brand new soccer ball, just what Luke had wanted. It was just the right size. It was the same ball he used in preschool, but this one was new. And, it was his.

Eli asked, "Do you like it Luke?" "Oh Eli. Thank you. It's just what I really wanted."

The two boys disappeared and soon the parents could hear the sound of kicking and running… and a lot of laughing. The boys were passing the new ball to each other, just as they had both learned at school. They didn't even hear Luke's mom call to them, "Please come inside so we can have some lunch and then some birthday cake."

Luke's dad came out the back door and watched the boys play. He was happy to see Luke and Eli playing so nicely together and didn't want them to stop. Finally, he called out, "Ok boys, time to eat. You can play again after lunch. We also have a birthday cake. I'm sure you want some of that."

Luke's mom had made Eli's favorite sandwich, Peanut Butter and Jelly. It was also Luke's favorite, especially when he had it with a big glass of cold milk. The boys were so hungry they finished their sandwiches before the parents had even started to eat their lunch, but they still sat in their chairs until everyone had finished. Luke's mom had said that as soon as lunch was over there would be birthday cake and both boys loved chocolate, so they waited very patiently. The cake soon arrived and Luke's dad lit the four candles since Luke was now four years old. Everyone sang happy birthday and when the singing was done, Luke was told to make a wish and not tell anyone. Then he could blow out the candles.

With the biggest breath he had ever taken, Luke thought to himself about his wish and blew out all four candles. He was so proud that he could do this. Everyone clapped and gave him a kiss. "I know I'm not supposed to tell you what I wished for, he said, but I want to anyway. I really, really like my new soccer ball, but my wish is that next year, when I'm 5, Eli can be with me again, because I love Eli."

CHAPTER 2
Age 5: The Uniform

"C'mon mom. I don't want to be late for soccer." It was the first night of soccer and all the boys and girls were told to report to Lincoln field at 6:00 to meet their coaches and get their shirts. Luke was hoping he would be on the blue team because blue was his favorite color. Luke's mom had bought him new soccer shoes and pads to protect his shins, but it was the shirt that Luke really wanted.

Luke and his mom drove to the field, parked the car and walked to the table where people were very busy giving instructions to the boys and girls. When it was Luke's turn, he started to smile and turned around to his mom. "I'm on the blue team, just like I hoped for."

Luke's mom walked him to the place on the field where the blue team was standing. The coach was Dr. Barnes, a very nice man who lived around the corner from Luke. Ryan Barnes, Dr. Barnes' son, was also on the blue team and this made Luke very happy because the boys were friends and played together after school. Luke's mom and Dr. Barnes talked for a few minutes and as she was leaving, Luke's mom gave Luke a big kiss, and said to Luke, "Have fun, be careful and I'll pick you up at 7:00."

When all nine children were present, Dr. Barnes introduced himself and asked them to line up by how tall they were. Luke was about in the middle. One boy, Zach, was very tall and was at one end. Another boy, Alex, was very short and was at the other end. The boy next to Luke,

Jordan, was almost exactly Luke's size. Jordan was in Luke's class but they didn't play with each other. Jordan was very shy and played by himself most of the time.

Dr. Barnes took out the blue shirts and handed one to each child. On the back of each shirt was a number from one to nine. Alex, who was the shortest, got number one while Zach, the tallest, got number nine. Luke got number five and Jordan got number six. Dr. Barnes told each child to put on the shirt, just to make sure it fit. They all were excited and put on their shirts. Everyone but Jordan. He looked very sad.

Luke said to Jordan, "What's the matter?" and Jordan answered, "My favorite number is 5 and that's what I really wanted."

Luke thought for a minute, took off his shirt and handed it to Jordan. "My favorite number is 6, so let's switch," Luke said, and the boys exchanged shirts. This made Jordan very happy and he said, "Thanks, Luke." Dr. Barnes was watching, but didn't say a word. He just smiled.

When practice was over, Luke's mom walked from the parking lot and met Dr. Barnes. The two talked for a minute. She took Luke by the hand and got into their car. Luke's mom turned to him and asked, "Did you have fun and do you like the children on your team?" Luke answered that he did and told her about the shirt that he had given to Jordan. Luke's mom smiled. She was very proud of what Luke had done and asked, "Why did you do that?" Luke answered, "It made Jordan happy and….well, my favorite number is 13 anyway." They both laughed.

CHAPTER 3
Age 6: Bangers and Mash

Luke knew it was the last day of school. He had been counting the days since the start of the month and now, it was really happening. Luke thought of all the wonderful things he would do on his summer vacation, but the thing he wanted to do the most was go to Soccer Camp. He was told about camp by his mom and dad and many of his friends from school were going to go. He kept looking at the pictures on the registration booklet and wondered what it would be like. He had heard that the coaches were all from England, even though Luke wasn't exactly sure where or what England was.

Each camper was told to wear shorts and tee shirts, their soccer shoes and shin pads, and to bring juice or water and a light snack. The camp was being held at Luke's school, only two blocks away, so Luke could either walk or ride his bike. Luke was excited. It made him feel grown up because there would be campers as old as 14 at the camp, doing the same things as he would be doing.

The first day of camp came very soon. It was a beautiful day, sunny, warm and not a cloud in the sky. Luke's mom made breakfast, waffles and fruit, Luke's favorite. As soon as he finished, Luke ran upstairs, brushed his teeth and came down, ready to leave. Luke's mom took out the sunscreen, rubbed it on Luke's face, arms and legs and looked at her son. He was growing up so fast, she thought to herself. She asked Luke if they could walk together to camp because she wanted to meet the camp coaches and make sure everything was just right. Luke said, "Ok, mom, but just this one time."

They arrived at the school and looked around. There were boys and girls everywhere. Luke wore his blue soccer shirt and the new soccer shoes his mom had bought yesterday. Some of the campers were really, really big Luke noticed. "They must be the 14 year olds," he thought. He wondered who his coach would be and if Luke would like him. He really liked Dr. Barnes and hoped he liked his coach just as much.

Over a microphone, the camp director spoke to all the campers and the parents. His name was Clyde and he sounded funny to Luke. Luke understood most of what Clyde said but some of the words didn't sound right. Many of the campers laughed when Clyde used the word football instead of soccer. He said that only in America did people call it soccer. He told the campers to find their coaches, all of whom were standing in a line at the middle of the field. Luke said good-bye to his mom, grabbed his water and snack and ran to a flag that said "Liverpool", the name of his group. Another funny sounding word he thought.

Standing with the flag was a tall, thin man with long blond hair. His nametag read Ian. Ian said hello to Luke and asked him to have a seat behind the flag. When the rest of the campers in the Liverpool group were seated, Ian welcomed them, told them what a wonderful week they would all have, and promised they would become better footballers by Friday. All the campers giggled when Ian spoke, especially when he said footballers.

The morning was spent learning everyone's names, how to stretch and, most importantly, how to play a few fun games with the soccer balls.

Ian watched closely as each child ran and kicked his or her soccer ball, blowing his whistle a few times to get everyone's attention. About halfway through the morning, Ian said there would be a 15-minute rest for the campers to take a long drink of water or juice and eat their snack.

During the break, Ian told the campers that he was 19 years old, lived in a small town in Wales and went to university in London. "How can you live in Whales?" asked Ari, one of the campers in the group.

Ian said it was pronounced the same as "Whales" but it was spelled WALES. Luke asked Ian if there were any Sharks in WALES. All the campers laughed and Ian said only when it was time to feed the Sharks with little boys wearing blue shirts and soccer shoes. Luke pretended not to hear Ian's answer.

The rest of the morning was spent with Ian showing the campers how to juggle a soccer ball on his head, feet and legs. Ian was able to keep the ball up at least 100 times without it hitting the ground. Luke kept trying and trying but could only go as high as three times. Ian said that was just super and that Luke should practice when he went home. "Maybe tomorrow you can do it 5 times and by Friday, you might go as high as 10." Luke said to himself, "I'm going to practice every afternoon and do 25 juggles."

At noon, Ian called the campers together, thanked them for being "Good blokes" and told them he was looking forward to another beautiful day tomorrow.

Luke's mom was waiting for Luke and he ran over and gave her a kiss. "I had the best time today. We learned about Sharks, WALES, Liver and Pools, and I was told I was a good bloke." Luke's mom just laughed and wondered exactly what he meant. That night at dinner, after his dad had come home from work, Luke went through his day at camp. His mom made spaghetti, Luke's favorite, and Luke had seconds. He told his dad that because he had run so much at camp, he might eat three or more servings.

As the dishes were being cleared, Luke turned to his mom and asked, "Do you think I can invite my coach, Ian, to come to dinner with us tomorrow?" His mom looked at his dad, smiled and said, "Of course you can. I will even make a special meal that will remind Ian of his home." Luke wondered what people who live in Wales ate. Do they like pizza, or chicken or hamburgers or…even fish?

The next morning, Luke rode his bike to camp, ran to Ian and juggled the ball 5 times. Ian smiled and said that when he was "a wee lad, just Luke's age, he could only juggle the ball 4 times." Luke said that was good, too, but he probably just needed to practice more. Ian chuckled. "Yes, I guess you're right."

The second day was a little warmer than the first and Ian made the campers take breaks more often. During the first break, Luke walked over to Ian and asked him if he would like to come to dinner at around 6:00. Ian thanked him and said he would love to come, but only if Luke promised to practice his juggling as soon as he finished his lunch at home. Luke smiled and kept wondering all morning what his mom would serve to make Ian feel at home.

At exactly 6:00, Ian rang the bell at Luke's house. Luke ran to the front door, opened it, shook Ian's hand, much to Ian's surprise, and invited him in. Both Luke's mom and dad soon came to the door and Ian shook their hands as well. Ian had brought a small bouquet of flowers and handed them to Luke's mom. "It's so nice to meet you, Ian," Luke's dad said. "We've heard so much about you. Please come in and make yourself comfortable."

The four people sat in the living room for about 15 minutes as they had ice tea, lemonade and some crackers with cheese that Luke's mom had prepared. When dinner was ready, they all moved into the dining room where Luke sat next to Ian. "My mom said she was going to make you something to make you feel at home," said Luke. Both Ian and Luke wondered what it might be.

A few minutes later, Luke's mom came into the dining room with a large platter that had some food Luke had never seen before. "What's that?" Luke cried out. "I've never seen that kind of food." Ian turned to Luke and said, "Luke, that's bangers and mash. We eat it at home all the time. My mum makes it, using a recipe that's been in our family for hundreds of years. This just looks wonderful. Thank you so much."

Luke's mom served the dinner, first to Ian and then to Luke who kept staring at it, wondering what it was. When everyone had been served, Ian took the first bite, turned to Luke's mom and said, "This tastes just as good as my mum's. It's my favorite meal. How did you know how to make it?"

"I googled it this afternoon," she said. "I'm glad you liked it." Luke was slow to take a bite, but after his first forkful, ate it almost as quickly as did Ian. He even asked his mom for more. They finished the meal with a big piece of cherry pie, topped with vanilla ice cream. Both Ian and Luke asked for seconds.

After the table was cleared and the dishes were washed and dried, Ian thanked Luke's family for a wonderful time. Luke walked with Ian to the front door where Ian told Luke how much he enjoyed dinner and that he was looking forward to camp tomorrow. Before he left, Ian turned to Luke and asked, "Luke, what is your favorite food?" "Spaghetti," said Luke, without even thinking. "I love spaghetti. I could eat it every night. I wish I had it for dinner tonight."

"It's my favorite, too," said Ian, much to Luke's surprise. "But, you said…" Ian interrupted him before he could finish his sentence. "I'll see you at camp tomorrow," Ian said as he walked down the front steps of Luke's house. Luke just smiled and closed the door.

CHAPTER 4

Age 7: The New Coach

THE PHONE RANG and Luke's mom answered. It was Mrs. Wilson, the wife of Luke's 7-year-old soccer team coach. "Oh, no," she said, "that's terrible," and continued to listen as the details of the accident were explained. "I'm so sorry. Is there anything I can do to help? 7 weeks? Well, let me speak with my husband, but he travels quite a bit and, besides, he doesn't know a lot about soccer. I'll call you back later."

She put the phone down and called up to Luke who was in his room. "Luke, can you please come down. I have something to tell you." "Sure, mom. I'll be right there," wondering what this could all be about.

When Luke came down the stairs, his mom turned to him and said "Luke, I have some bad news for you. Your coach, Mr. Wilson has been in a serious accident. I just spoke with Mrs. Wilson and it looks like he won't be able to coach your team this season. I'm sorry, but he has to stay in the hospital for at least a few weeks and then rest at his house for a few more."

Luke didn't know what to say. He just stood there, motionless, until his mom gave him a big hug that caused him to cry, just a little. "He'll be ok, Luke," she said. "He just can't be your coach this year." Luke pulled away from his mom. "Who will be the coach, mom? We need a coach."

His mom didn't answer at first. Finally, she said, "Someone will coach the team. It just might take some time to find the right person." Luke went back to his room but, as he climbed the stairs, his mom heard him say very softly, "What will we do? Practice is in 2 days. I hope we can find a new coach."

Luke's dad came home at his usual time, around 5:30. He gave his wife a kiss, looked in on Jack who was taking a nap and asked, "Well, anything exciting today?" a question he asked every time he came home, anticipating the usual answer of "no, nothing exciting." Today, however, was different. Luke's mom explained the call she had just received and said, "Do you think you might be the coach?" They had had this conversation before. Luke's dad was an engineer and traveled a lot, inspecting generators all across the country. He was often away from home for 3 or 4 days at a time and had politely refused to be the coach in any sport because of his schedule.

"I don't think I can do it," he said. "You know how often I'm not here, and, besides I don't know anything about soccer." As he was speaking, Luke came into the room and said, "Did mom tell you what happened to Mr. Wilson? He can't be our coach because of the accident. I hope we can find a coach because the next practice is in 2 days."

"Well, Luke," his dad said, "I'm sure someone will be able to do this," and, with that comment, Luke walked out the back door and started kicking his soccer ball into the net his dad had made for him during the summer.

"I know about your schedule," his mom said, "but this would mean so much to Luke if you could be the coach. Is there any way you could arrange things so you could be there, at least most of the time? I'm sure you can find someone to take your place if you really cannot make it." Luke's dad thought for a moment and answered, "Let me check things at work. Maybe I can do it…but no promises."

At dinner, Luke hardly said a word. He just kept wondering who would be the coach. He barely touched his spaghetti, his favorite food, and turned down dessert. He knew not to ask his dad if he could be the coach. This conversation always ended the same way, with Luke being disappointed when his dad said he couldn't because of his work. Luke asked to be excused and went back to his room without a sound. His mom followed him upstairs, leaving dad to do the dishes and to take care of Jack. Nothing more was said that night about the coaching.

The next day Luke came home from school and was met in the driveway by his mom who was a middle school teacher in the next town. "So, Luke how was your day?" she asked. Luke said it was fine, but his mom knew it wasn't. Luke usually could not stop talking about what he had learned that day so she knew he was unhappy. "Still thinking about your coach?" she asked, knowing exactly what the problem was. "I guess so," he answered and walked into the house.

Luke's dad was late and when he came home, everyone had already eaten dinner. Luke's mom joined him at the table. "I have something to tell the family. Can you please ask Luke to come down?"

Luke walked slowly into the room, gave his dad a very light hug and sat down. "I have an announcement to make," he said. "I've found the new coach!" Luke's eyes lit up and asked, "Is it Mr. Phillips? He played soccer in college and is always showing us tricks he can do with the soccer ball. I hope it's him," Luke said. "No, it's not Mr. Phillips." Luke's mom knew what was coming and tried to hide her smile.

"It's me, Luke. I'm the new coach. How does that make you feel?" Luke didn't know what to say. This was the first time his dad would be the coach in any sport. "But dad," Luke said, "I didn't think you knew anything about soccer. How can you be the coach?" His dad looked right at Luke and said, "I guess I'll have to learn very, very quickly. I might need a teacher, maybe someone like you Luke. Ok?"

Luke walked over to his dad and, this time, gave him the biggest, tightest squeeze he could. "You'll do great, dad. I can't wait to tell the other kids. But, you know, you'll have to buy some soccer shoes. You can't coach us in your running shoes."

The next day at school, Luke told his friends about the new coach. He was very proud of his dad but wondered what it would be like at practice. One boy, Connor, made Luke feel bad when he said, "Luke, your dad doesn't know anything about soccer. How can he be the coach?" Luke wondered the same thing but soon forgot about it when his teacher, Miss O'Brien, asked him a question about the story the class had finished reading.

The day passed very slowly but the final bell rang and Luke raced home to get ready for practice. At 5:00, his mom gave him dinner and, a few minutes later, his dad walked in. His dad was holding a small box under his arm. Luke knew right away what it was. His dad opened the box and took out a shiny, new pair of soccer shoes. "Are these ok?" he asked. "They're perfect, dad," Luke replied. His dad then opened a small bag and pulled out a silver whistle. Luke smiled. "Now you're really the coach. But you are going to change out of your suit, aren't you?"

His dad went to his room and came back a few minutes later wearing a t-shirt and shorts…and, of course the new shoes and whistle. "Ok, let's go," his dad said. Luke was still excited…and, a little nervous.

They drove to the field and Luke's dad met the boys and girls. All the parents were there, too, and Luke's dad spoke with them for a few minutes. After the parents left, Luke's dad introduced himself and made sure he knew each child by name. He asked them to line up, just as Mr. Wilson did, and had them do some stretching and running around the field…just like Mr. Wilson did. In fact, the practice was the same as the practices that Mr. Wilson ran.

The hour passed very quickly and Luke's dad finally blew his whistle, telling the children that practice was over and he would see them again on Saturday morning. Luke was happy. His dad had done a wonderful job as coach. In fact, each child on the team told Luke the same thing. Even Connor.

Luke's mom was waiting for them as they drove up the driveway. "Well, how was practice?" she asked. "Great," said Luke, ran to his dad, and gave him a hug. Once Luke was in the house, she turned to Luke's dad and asked the same question. "Just fine," he said. Everything ran just as Mrs. Wilson said it would."

"Mrs. Wilson?" his mom asked? "Why Mrs. Wilson?"

"Well, on the way home I stopped at the hospital to see how Mr. Wilson was. He's doing fine and should be home in a few weeks. Before I left, Mrs. Wilson and I left the room. She handed me a piece of paper that had the entire practice schedule."

"Why did she have the schedule?" Luke's mom asked. Luke's dad smiled just a bit and said, "It seems that Mr. Wilson doesn't know much about soccer either, but Mrs. Wilson used to be a high school soccer coach. They worked as a team. She wrote everything out for her husband since she could never make the practices because of her job. I guess you could say that it takes a good team to make a good team."

Luke came back outside and overheard them talking about a good team. "We're a good team, dad, aren't we? Especially with you as our coach." "Yes, Luke," his dad said. "Both at soccer practice and at home with your mom and brother."

Everyone laughed.

CHAPTER 5
Age 8: The Injury

THE FIELD AND goals had grown, and so had the children. Each team now played with 11 players, not 8, as they had done during the past few years. For the first time, there was a real referee and a small scoreboard. Before this year, no one had officially kept score, but the players always seemed to know exactly who had won and who had lost. The colored t-shirts of the past were replaced with uniforms that looked like those worn by the professional teams shown on television.

Luke was on Arsenal, a team that played in England and was nicknamed the "Gunners". Although his uniform was not blue, Luke's favorite color, he loved his new shirt that had a picture of a cannon on the front.

His coach was Mr. Edwards. Mr. Edwards had been a coach for a number of years. He had coached his older son, Ben, for 5 years and now it was his turn to coach his younger son, Dylan. Luke didn't know Dylan. He lived on the other side of town and went to a different school. There were only two other boys on Luke's new team that he knew, but he was still looking forward to a new season. He just loved playing soccer.

On the first night of practice, Mr. Edwards asked each child to say whom they were and what position they might like to play. A few of the children had never played soccer before and didn't know what to answer. When it was Luke's turn, he said he liked playing either striker or midfielder, but any position except goalkeeper would be fine.

There were 12 boys and 2 girls on the team. After stretching for a few minutes, Mr. Edwards lined them all up and had them sprint across the field to see who was the fastest. The girls came in first and second. Luke came in third, but was only one-step behind.

After a quick water break, the children started the formal practice activities. They were taught to dribble around some orange cones, and to break into pairs and throw the ball to each other so they could learn how to trap and head the ball. Luke was paired with Alex, the girl who was the fastest. Dylan was paired with Jennifer, the other girl.

10 minutes later, Mr. Edwards asked everyone to switch partners. Luke and Dylan wound up together. It was easy to see that they were the two best players on the team, but they didn't seem to play together very well. Dylan kept telling Luke that he already knew how to do all this since he practiced a lot with his older brother. Luke just tried to keep up with Dylan but he was not very happy with his partner.

For the last 15 minutes of practice, Mr. Edwards said there would be a scrimmage. He divided the children into 2 teams, with Luke on one and Dylan on the other. They used small goals without goalkeepers and played until one team scored three times.

After a few minutes, the score was tied 2 to 2 with Luke and Dylan each scoring twice. The next goal would win. With less than a minute to go, Dylan stole the ball from one of the players, raced down the field and kicked the ball towards the open net, only to have Luke kick it away at the very last moment. Luke then kicked the ball as hard as he could in the opposite direction. It kept bouncing and rolling until it reached the other goal, finally stopping inside the net.

Mr. Edwards blew his whistle and told all the players what a wonderful job they had done. "I'll see you all on Thursday," he said. "Please make sure you practice. It looks like we will have a great team this year, especially if Luke continues to score so many goals." Luke was smiling but couldn't take his eyes off Dylan who looked very unhappy.

On the drive home, Luke told his mom about practice, especially the part about Dylan. "Maybe Dylan is used to being the best player. This might be the first time someone is as good as he is," she said. "Maybe he thinks his dad now prefers you to him. That certainly would make him unhappy. Or, maybe he's just having a bad day. Let's give it some time." Luke thought his mom was very smart. She always knew exactly what to say to make him feel better and this time was no exception.

Thursday's practice was much the same except when it came time to scrimmage, Mr. Edwards put Dylan and Luke on the same team. As soon as the game started, Dylan kept dribbling the ball himself and wouldn't pass it to any of his teammates, especially not to Luke. Dylan scored two goals almost immediately. He kept smiling at his dad who just shook his head while his teammates yelled at him to pass them the ball.

Mr. Edwards blew his whistle and said there was a rule change. Before either team could score a goal, every player would have to touch the ball at least once. This would force Dylan to pass the ball.

Play resumed and things did get a little better and Luke would end up scoring the next goal. Dylan was as unhappy as he was at the last practice and just walked to his dad's car without saying goodbye to the rest of the team.

The season started the following Saturday and Arsenal won its first game, 3-2, with both Dylan and Luke each scoring a goal. They won their next two games so, by the fourth week, they were tied for first place. Dylan seemed to have calmed down a little, but he still never passed the ball to Luke, even when Luke was open. On that fourth week, Arsenal was playing Barcelona with both teams trying to stay undefeated.

The game was very even and then, suddenly, Luke was down on the ground, holding his right ankle, tears running down his cheeks. Mr. Edwards ran onto the field, as did Luke's mom and dad. Luckily, Dr. Ramsey's son, Evan, was on Barcelona and she raced onto the field to see what had happened.

After a few minutes, Mr. Edwards and Luke's dad carried Luke off the field, an ice pack wrapped around his swollen ankle. Dr. Ramsey told Luke's parents to go to the hospital immediately. She said it might be a severe sprain. Luke's mom asked Luke if it hurt, to which he said it did. Luke then asked her if he might not be able to play the next game, to which she said, "Probably not."

Luke didn't say another word until they arrived at the hospital. The doctor at the Emergency Room spoke to the family after the x-rays were read. Luke's ankle had a very severe sprain, but there were no broken bones. However, the doctor said, "I'm sorry, but he'll need crutches for a while and his activities must be limited. And…I'm very sorry to say, no soccer for at least 4 weeks."

Luke's heart sank and went right to bed after his dad carried him up to his room. "I can't let my team down," he said, trying to fight back the tears. His dad kissed him good night and walked out of the room. As he was leaving, he turned to Luke and said, "You'll think of some way to help them. I know you will."

Mr. Edwards called a few minutes after Luke had fallen asleep, asking how Luke was feeling. Luke's mom told him about the sprain and that Luke would likely miss the next 4 weeks, and it might be even longer. Mr. Edwards asked her to tell him how much the team would miss him and wished him a speedy recovery.

Tuesday night came very quickly for Luke. He had spent most of the past few days resting and learning how to use the crutches. It wasn't easy but he kept trying. His friends at school helped him by carrying his books and opening doors for him. He was certainly the center of attention, even if he wished he wasn't.

At around 5:45, Luke turned to his mom and asked her if she would drive him to soccer practice. She was surprised by his request but understood why he had asked. "If you really want to go, of course I'll take you," she replied. "What are you going to do there?" Luke wasn't exactly sure of the answer but said, "Maybe I can help."

20 minutes later, Luke opened the door of his mom's car, got up on his crutches and hobbled to where the team was practicing. The team stopped what they were doing and everyone ran over to see Luke and his ankle. "Does it hurt? Can you go to school? When can you come back to play?" The questions kept coming. Even Dylan came over to see the ankle but didn't say a word.

Mr. Edwards walked over and joined the team that surrounded Luke.

"Luke," he said, "I guess even a sprained ankle couldn't keep you away. Are you here to watch or would you like to help me?" he asked. "I could use an assistant and you might be just the person. Are you interested?"

Before Mr. Edwards could finish his question, Luke yelled out, "Yes, I am. What can I do?" and followed his coach to the bench next to the practice field.

"Luke," he said, "I need you to do two things. The first thing is to keep the time so I know what activity we should be doing." He handed Luke his watch and explained the practice schedule. "The second thing might be a little harder. I want you to cheer your teammates every time they pass the ball. Especially Dylan."

Luke thought for a minute, took a deep breath and answered, "Of course I can do that." Inside, however, he wondered how Dylan would react. Dylan was already looking a little angry, watching how much time Luke was spending with his dad.

At 6:30, Mr. Edwards divided the group into 2 teams and they started playing against each other. Every time someone made a pass, Luke would clap his hands and yell encouragement. He yelled the loudest and clapped the hardest when Dylan passed the ball. At first, Dylan just stared at Luke, but soon, he started to smile. He smiled even wider when his dad clapped his hands every time Dylan made a good pass.

After about 20 minutes, Mr. Edwards blew his whistle and told the players what an excellent practice they had. He then walked over and spoke with Luke's mom who was waiting near the field. She waved to Luke as she got in her car and drove away, leaving Luke a bit surprised. Mr. Edwards turned to Luke and asked, "Would you like to join Dylan and me for ice cream? Your mom said it was okay."

Luke thought about his answer for less than a second. "I love ice cream, especially mint chocolate chip with rainbow sprinkles. Thank you for asking me."

"That's my favorite, too," said Dylan, standing a few feet away. The two boys looked at each other and laughed as they walked to Mr. Edward's car. "Can I help you with your crutches, Luke?" asked Dylan. "Thanks," said Luke as they drove to the Dairy Barn, the best ice cream place in town.

Ten minutes later, they arrived and found an empty booth near the door. The server took their order and soon brought two large bowls of mint chocolate chip ice cream for the boys and a hot fudge sundae for Mr. Edwards. The server also brought out a large container, filled with rainbow sprinkles and placed it in front of Dylan, seated nearest the door. He filled his bowl and, before Luke could say a word, passed the container of sprinkles to him. Luke and Mr. Edwards just clapped their hands and smiled.

CHAPTER 6
Age 9: The Move

As soon as Luke walked in the house, he knew something was wrong. He had been playing most of the afternoon with his friend Kyle who lived across the street. They always used Kyle's computer to play video games and then would go outside to kick Luke's new soccer ball into a large net that Kyle's dad had made.

Kyle was the goalie on Luke's team and, following their usual routine, the two boys took turns shooting penalty kicks. Kyle was very tall and could almost jump high enough to touch the cross bar on a regulation goal.

Luke's mom and dad were sitting in the living room. Jack sat with Luke's mom and he did not look very happy. "Luke," his dad said, "we have something to tell you." Luke just froze. He could see that this was going to be big. "Is anyone sick?" he asked. "Is Jack ok?"

"Yes, everyone's fine," his dad announced, "but we do have something to tell you and we hope you'll like it. It's not bad," his dad continued. Luke ran over and gave his mom a hug.

"I have a new job," his dad said. "It's a promotion but it means we will be moving, probably before the school year begins."

Luke's family lived in New Jersey, near Philadelphia. His favorite team was the Eagles, but he also liked the Phillies and the Union, the local professional soccer team. Luke's dad had taken him to a few games and Luke proudly wore his Union jersey whenever he could. Luke had so many questions, the first one being, "What's a promotion?"

Luke's dad started to explain but all Luke could think about was how much he would miss his school and friends. He also wondered if they played soccer in his new town. "Where will we live?" Luke asked.

"Well, we're not exactly sure yet," his dad replied. "My new job is in Washington DC so we will either live in Virginia or Maryland."

"Can I still wear my Eagles and Union jerseys?" Luke asked. His mom gave him a kiss on the cheek and said, "Of course you can. You can wear anything you want."

Luke still didn't feel very comfortable and spent the rest of the afternoon laying on his bed, just wondering about lots and lots of things.

During the next few weeks, Luke and his family took weekend drives to see places where they might live. Most of the houses were bigger than their old house but they all seemed nice. And, the best part was that there were always kids Luke's age playing outside, either shooting baskets, riding bikes or throwing and catching a ball with a funny looking net at the end of a long stick. Luke asked his dad what this was. "It's called Lacrosse," his dad answered. "It's very popular in this area. Maybe you would like to learn how to play." Luke wasn't sure and just shrugged his shoulders.

Luke's family finally decided on a large red brick house with a long driveway that was near a park. The house was in Virginia, just a few miles from the White House in Washington, DC. Luke knew that the President lived in the White House because he learned about it in school.

Luke and Jack were both excited and ran upstairs to claim their rooms. "I like this room because it has lots of windows and is painted blue, my favorite color," said Luke. Jack just sat on the floor of his new room and did not say a word.

School was starting in less than 2 weeks when Luke's family moved into their new house. When they arrived, the large moving van was already parked on the street and three strong men were bringing things into the house. A few neighbors were standing in the driveway and welcomed Luke's mom and dad to the neighborhood. There was also a boy, just about Luke's age, juggling a soccer ball in front of the house.

He stopped his juggling when Luke got out of his car, walked over to Luke and said, "Welcome to Virginia. My name is Luke, but people call me LJ because my middle name is Jason. I'm the best soccer player in the whole third grade." Luke started to laugh. "My name is also Luke and I was the best soccer player in the whole third grade last year…in New Jersey. I guess it's good that people call me Luke. Otherwise they'd get us confused." Both boys laughed and started kicking the soccer ball to each other. "I think I'm going to like living here," thought Luke.

Almost 2 weeks later, the yellow school bus arrived in front of Luke's house. Luke and LJ climbed the steps and said hello to their driver, Sonny, as he called himself. Luke wondered why a grown man would be called Sonny. Once seated, LJ introduced Luke to all his friends, telling them that Luke was the best soccer player in his grade in New Jersey. Luke just smiled and wondered what his new school would be like… and, how he would like his new soccer team and soccer coach.

After a short 10-minute drive, the bus stopped in front of Lincoln Elementary School. It was about the same size as his old school in New Jersey, but it looked much newer. Luke could feel his stomach get tight as he followed LJ to their classroom. It was the first time he ever felt this way and wondered how long it might last. He didn't like the feeling at all.

Luke found his seat in the back of the second row, next to a boy named Peter. His teacher, Mrs. Johnson, started to call out each child's name. When it came to announcing Luke, she paused and said that Luke had just moved from New Jersey and hoped that everyone would welcome him to his new school. Peter, who was much bigger than Luke was and had a reputation for being a bully, said in a very low voice that only Luke could hear, "Hey, Puke. New Jersey stinks." Luke pretended not to hear him but the words just made his stomach get tight again.

The rest of the morning was uneventful. Luke ate lunch with LJ and a few of LJ's friends. They had all heard about what a good soccer player Luke was. Luke tried to listen but his eyes kept looking at Peter who was sitting at a table all by himself. At 2:00, the class went to the gym where

Mrs. Reynolds met them. Mrs. Reynolds said that because it was the first day of school, the class could choose what they would like to do.

Almost immediately, LJ yelled out "Soccer." Most of the class agreed so Mrs. Reynolds asked LJ to be the captain of one team and to choose who would be the other captain. LJ chose Luke and the two boys were told to start picking their teams with LJ choosing first.

All the children started to raise their hands, yelling, "Pick me, pick me." All, that is, except Peter who was standing by himself. LJ chose Matt, one of his best friends who also lived on Luke's block. Luke thought for a minute, looked around the room and said "Peter."

As most of the class started to laugh, Peter came forward, didn't say a word to Luke, and lined up behind him.

After the rest of the teams were chosen, Mrs. Reynolds gave instructions. The game would have two 10-minute periods with a five minute rest in between. The captains would decide the positions and the players would switch between offense and defense during the break. Luke made sure that Peter's position was near his.

At the end of the first period, the game was tied 1-1 with LJ and Luke scoring goals for their teams. Peter only touched the ball twice, since none of the players on his own team would pass him the ball. With about two minutes left in the game, Luke stole the ball from the other team and dribbled down the field. The only player from the other team who was in front of him was Chris, the last player chosen because he ran very, very slowly. Luke knew he could dribble around Chris, but, as he got closer to the goal, he yelled at the top of his voice, "PETER!" To Peter's surprise, Luke passed him the ball and Peter kicked it into the goal. All of Peter's teammates surrounded him and patted him on the back. For the first time that day, Peter smiled. So did Luke.

At dinner that night, Luke told his mom and dad about his first day of school. They had so many questions. His mom finally asked if he had made any friends. Luke stopped eating his spaghetti, thought for a minute and finally said, "Well, I'm pretty sure I made at least one."

CHAPTER 7
Age 10: The Travel Team

THE FIRST YEAR in Virginia went very quickly. Luke and LJ continued to be best friends. Jack started kindergarten at the same school and rode the yellow bus under Luke's watchful eye. The family had spent the last 3 weeks back in New Jersey, visiting Luke's cousins who lived at the Jersey shore. Luke missed them already, especially Eli, and wished they lived closer. Luke had attended a soccer camp in July, very similar to the one in New Jersey. He couldn't wait for school to start because that meant it was also the beginning of a new soccer season.

Luke had just turned 10 and his mom and dad agreed to let him try out for the travel team. The main travel team consisted of the best players from their town. There were tryouts and Luke heard that it was very difficult to be chosen for this team. He had practiced his juggling, dribbling and shooting every day, both with LJ and with his dad. He was a little nervous because he had never tried out for a team and was afraid he might not make it. There would be another team for the 10 year olds who didn't make this team, but Luke had his heart set on the main team.

Tryouts for the 10 year olds were held on the first Saturday in September at his school. Luke thought this was great because it made him feel very comfortable. LJ felt the same way. The coach of the travel team was Mr. Erickson. Mr. Erickson had been a college soccer player and was hired to coach the team. For the first time, Luke was going to have a coach who didn't have a child on the team.

Each child was handed a practice shirt with a number printed on the back. Mr. Erickson spoke to the players and parents, explaining how the team would be chosen and what everyone should expect during the season. He said they would practice twice a week, play games every Sunday afternoon and take part in two tournaments. One tournament would be in Virginia and the other would be in New Jersey. Luke was excited at the thought of going back to New Jersey. Maybe he would be playing against some of his old friends. Maybe even his cousin, Eli.

The practice lasted for two and a half hours. Luke enjoyed most of it but did not like all the stretching that Mr. Ericson had them do. He kept thinking, "When are we actually going to play?" His friend, LJ, stood next to Luke and both of them started to giggle when Mr. Erickson made them walk on the outside of their soccer shoes. They both felt like ducks, just waddling around the field.

After stretching, the players were told to run around the field twice, but not as fast as they could go. Luke loved to run and kept up the pace at the front. LJ stayed behind and had to stop for a minute to catch his breath. He had never run this much before and didn't like it at all.

Mr. Erickson kept watching and made some notes on his clipboard. The next 30 minutes saw the players playing small-sided games using cones as goals. Luke liked this except when his team played LJ's and the friends had to guard each other.

A 10-minute water break came next, Luke and LJ stood together, discussing what they had just done, and wondering what would be coming. Mr. Erickson had the players line up at the end line and, on his whistle, had them sprint to midfield. LJ was the fastest with Luke following him a few steps behind.

They had to repeat this four times and by the last race, most of the players, including LJ, were walking and holding their sides, trying to catch their breath. Not Luke. He was only one of six players who could actually run every sprint. Again, Mr. Erickson made some notes. The last 30 minutes were spent on the big field. There were 33 players divided into 3 teams, one wearing blue shirts, a second wearing yellow and the third wearing green.

Both Luke and LJ were on the blue team. The first 10 minutes had the blue and the yellow teams play. This was followed by the blue and green teams and finally the yellow and green. As the last game ended, Mr. Erickson blew his whistle, thanked the players and the parents and said that he would call everyone by Wednesday evening, saying whether they had made the team.

Luke and LJ walked off the field together and didn't say a word as they climbed into the back of Luke's car. "Well," Luke's mom asked, "how was it?" "OK," said Luke. "Yeah, it was really hard," said LJ. "There were 33 kids and only 16 can make the team. I sure hope we both will be picked." The boys didn't say another word on the ride home.

That night at dinner, Luke's dad asked the same question, as did his mom. "So, how was the practice?" to which Luke replied, "It was much harder than I thought it would be. I really hope both LJ and I make the team," and with that, Luke just finished his spaghetti and asked to be excused.

Wednesday night came very slowly, or it just seemed that way to Luke. Each day at school was spent thinking about how great it would be to be chosen…and how awful it would feel not to make the team. He and LJ didn't discuss it at all.

Finally, at around 7:30, Luke's cell phone rang. It was Mr. Erickson. Luke's heart started to beat so hard that he thought it would come right through his chest. "Hi Luke," the voice on the other end said. "I have some very good news. You're on the team. We start practice tomorrow night, 6:00 sharp. I'll see you then." Before Luke could say another word, the call ended. "Wow," Luke said to himself. "I wanted to ask if LJ made the team, too."

Luke immediately dialed LJ to find out the answer. The phone was busy and Luke was wondering if Mr. Erickson was talking to LJ. He called twice more. There was no answer either time so Luke texted LJ, asking if he had heard from Mr. Erickson. A minute later came a very short message: "I didn't make it." Luke started to cry and just texted back, "I'm sorry." LJ wouldn't answer his phone for the rest of the evening.

Luke's mom and dad, who had heard Luke's phone ring, came into his room and saw the tears rolling down Luke's cheeks. "I'm sorry you didn't make the team," his mom said.

"I did make the team," Luke replied, much to the astonishment of both parents. "Then why are you crying?" came the question from his dad. "We don't understand."

Luke simply sat down on his bed and stared at the blue practice shirt he had worn to the tryout. "LJ didn't make the team. If he isn't on the team, I don't want to play either. We're best friends. I know LJ is upset because he won't answer his phone. I'm going to call Mr. Erickson and tell him." Luke's parents just gave him a big hug.

Luke wasn't able to sleep that night, wondering why LJ didn't make the team and thinking about what he would say to his best friend at school on Thursday. He just knew he wasn't going to play. He reached for his phone and started to dial Mr. Erickson.

LJ wasn't on the bus the next morning. Luke was sure he was too upset to come to school and tell the other kids he didn't make the team. As he left the bus, Luke saw LJ's car pull up in front of the school. LJ got out, ran over to Luke gave him a high five and screamed at the top of his lungs "I made it! I made it."

Luke was stunned. "What happened," he asked? "One of the boys changed his mind and decided he didn't want to play soccer this year. Mr. Erickson called me back this morning and said I was next on the list. That's why I missed the bus," answered LJ. "Isn't that great?"

All Luke could think about was how close he came last night to telling Mr. Erickson that he had changed his mind too. Luke just smiled, picked up his backpack and walked through the front door of the school with his best friend, never to discuss the matter again.

CHAPTER 8
Age 11: The Decision

Luke couldn't believe it. He kept staring at the mirror in his room. The practice jersey he had worn to last year's tryouts stopped short at his belly button. He hadn't worn the shirt for almost 9 months and, now, he realized just how much he had grown. He was well aware that his voice was changing, causing him to sound silly in class when his teacher asked him to read something aloud. He knew he had grown. Just not quite this much.

At breakfast, Luke's dad asked if he would like to go with him to the local driving range to hit some golf balls. Luke's dad loved golf and had asked Luke a few times to go but, each time, Luke was either at soccer practice or at LJ's, playing video games. Today, however, Luke said yes.

Luke ran upstairs and brought down two junior clubs that he had received recently as birthday gifts. This would be the first time Luke could use them and was excited at the thought of seeing how far he could hit a ball and spending the morning with his dad. His dad's new job took him away for days at a time and father and son rarely were on the same schedule.

Luke's dad put his clubs in the trunk of their car, along with Luke's two clubs and in 15 minutes arrived at the local driving range. They purchased a large bucket of range balls and split them into smaller buckets so each would have their own. Luke had never actually hit a golf ball so his dad asked him to watch for a few minutes, explaining where to stand and how to swing the club. Luke wondered how difficult this could be since the club was very big and the ball was so tiny.

Finally, it was Luke's turn to hit. He took a few practice swings, then moved closer to the ball and took a real swing. He missed the ball completely. In fact, he took three more swings, missing the ball each time.

"That's ok," Luke's dad said. "Keep your eye on the ball and try not to swing so hard." On the fifth try, Luke hit the ball perfectly, causing it to land close to the 100-yard marker. "That's great. Try a few more. Just remember, don't swing too hard," his dad exclaimed. All Luke could think about was how great it felt to spend time with his dad.

On the drive home, Luke's dad asked when spring soccer practice would start. Luke had played during the summer, the fall and the winter and hesitated to answer his dad's question. The summer had been the highlight because his team had played in the same big tournament in New Jersey, as did his cousin Eli's team, even though their teams never met.

"I think in about 2 weeks," Luke finally said. "But I'm not sure if I want to play in the spring."

"Is there a particular reason?" his dad asked to which Luke replied, "It's not as much fun as it used to be. I was wondering if I should be doing something different. I still like it, especially since LJ and I are on the same team. I just don't know. What do you think?"

Luke's dad didn't answer right away. "Let's talk about this with mom when we get home," he said. His dad usually gave that answer to important questions.

After putting away their clubs, Luke and his dad went to the backyard and found Luke's mom working in the garden. She loved her garden, took every opportunity to plant flowers, and keep everything looking perfect. "We'd like your opinion on something," Luke's dad said. "It's pretty important and we're sorry to interrupt what you're doing."

The three of them walked into the house and Luke's mom poured glasses of lemonade. Jack, who was watching cartoons in the family room, joined them in the kitchen for this family meeting. Luke, once again, explained that he wasn't sure about playing soccer in the spring. His mom wasn't surprised. She knew that Luke's schedule was beginning to take up all his time and wondered when he might decide to give something up. Although she knew that Luke loved soccer, it did take up the biggest amount of his time. She also had read that more and more young children are "burnt out" by playing a sport year round so Luke's situation was actually encouraging to her.

"What would you do instead of soccer?" his mom asked. "Maybe take golf lessons," Luke replied, "or karate."

"Why don't you take a few days to think about this," his dad said. "You might feel different tomorrow."

That night Luke made a list, putting all the things, good and bad about his decision. At the top of the list was playing with his teammates, all of whom had become Luke's friends. Luke hated the idea of not seeing them for the next few months. Learning a new activity was next, followed by spending more time with his family and being able to have Sundays off so he could just play with his neighborhood friends. He also wrote down that he could watch Jack play soccer, now that Jack was old enough to play in the town league. The last thing Luke wrote was wondering if skipping spring soccer might cause him never to want to play soccer again. A very, very difficult decision for an 11-year-old boy to make.

The next day during recess, Luke told LJ about his decision. He had made up his mind that he would skip spring soccer and take golf lessons. LJ couldn't believe that his best friend was quitting. He couldn't decide whether he felt angry or sad. The only thing he could think of saying was "That really stinks" and walked away.

Luke just stood there, frozen…and disappointed. He thought LJ might not like this decision but he really hoped LJ would understand.

LJ would not even make eye contact with Luke the rest of the day and sat far away from him on the bus going home. Luke just stared out the bus window and wondered if he had made the right decision. It was the longest 15-minute ride he had ever taken.

The bus finally stopped in front of Luke's house and Luke and LJ got out. The silence continued and Luke slowly walked up his driveway, only to be met by his mom who had arrived home just a few minutes earlier.

She took one look at Luke's face and knew something was wrong. And, she had a good idea what it was. "I'm guessing you made up your mind and told LJ," she said. "Is that why you're looking so upset?" Luke just kept walking, not even stopping to give his mom a kiss.

At dinner that night, Luke hardly touched his food. He barely said a word. Finally, he turned to his dad and asked, "Do you think I made the right choice? I don't feel very good about this. What would you do?"

"Well," his dad said in a very soft voice. "I would do what you think when you first open your eyes in the morning. It's always better to wait. Remember last year when you were going to call Mr. Erickson?"

After dinner, Luke helped his mom with the dishes and asked her the same questions. "I like what your dad told you, Luke. You know, he couldn't make up his mind about taking that new job a few years ago and just waited until the morning to decide. It doesn't always work. We're all different," his mom replied. "I'm pretty sure you'll make the right decision for you," she continued and kissed him on the cheek as he loaded the last plate into the dishwasher.

Sleep did not come easily to Luke that night. He tossed, turned, and kept looking at the clock next to his bed. He kept thinking about LJ and the rest of the team. He also thought about how much he liked spending time with his dad and learning to play golf would make that time even more special. At around 11:00 he drifted off, still wondering what to do.

The alarm interrupted his sleep at the usual 6:30 am time. He was tired and waited almost a full minute before opening his eyes. His face was still buried in the pillow but managed to turn slightly to the right, his one eye half open, the other still shut tight. He kept waiting for a voice to tell him what to do.

It came from his brother, Jack. "WAKE UP LUKE! YOU'LL BE LATE!" Not exactly what Luke wanted to hear. Still no answer.

LJ was already waiting at the bus stop just as Luke ran out of the house. "Come on, sleepyhead," LJ yelled. "You'll miss the bus." Luke just thought to himself, "Maybe LJ isn't mad at me anymore," as the two boys climbed aboard.

They sat together in the very last row but didn't say another word.

In fact, most of the day passed and still nothing from LJ. Nothing, that is, until afternoon recess. As they stood near the corner of the large fenced yard, LJ finally spoke. "I'm excited for you," he said. "I'm sorry I seemed angry when you told me about not wanting to play spring soccer, but I think I understand. I guess I thought you didn't want to be friends anymore and I was more upset than angry. If we really are good friends, then we should be happy for each other, no matter what."

Luke just listened. "I was being selfish," said LJ. "I think it sounds great that you'll learn to play golf and spend time with your dad. Maybe I can take lessons during the summer and we can play together. Even better, maybe you and your dad can play with my dad and me. That would really be neat, especially if they let us drive the golf carts." They both laughed and started kicking the soccer ball until it was time to come inside.

CHAPTER 9

Age 12: Middle School, Girls and the Rest of Life

"I'M A LITTLE nervous," Luke confided to his mom. "What if I don't like Middle School? I heard the teachers are really strict and there's tons of homework every night." The two of them had been having this conversation on a regular basis for the past week so Luke knew exactly what his mom would say.

"Well," his mom said, "you could stay home with me and be home schooled. That would be fun, wouldn't it?" Luke loved his mom, but the thought of not seeing his friends and being with his mom all day was a little too much for a growing boy of 12 to take. "Thanks for the offer mom," Luke blurted out. "Maybe Middle School won't be so bad after all." The subject was never brought up again.

On Tuesday morning, Luke met LJ on the corner and waited for their bus to arrive. Luke had pleaded with his mom not to wait with him. He was surprised when she agreed. There were seven or eight other children waiting for the bus when he arrived. Boys, girls, short, tall, happy, sad. Luke couldn't believe how big a few of them were, especially the girls. He was even more amazed that a few of the girls didn't look like the girls he knew from his elementary school. He couldn't take his eyes off them, as much as he tried.

The ride to school seemed to take forever. LJ and Luke tried to hide their nervousness but it was obvious to both that life would never be the same. More scared than excited, they stepped off the bus into a completely new world.

A few of their friends from elementary school ran to meet them and the group slowly walked through the front door, looking for something called a Homeroom. During orientation, Luke learned that he would have different teachers during the day and the first stop would always be Homeroom. LJ and Luke were assigned to different rooms and, as the boys separated, they agreed to meet at lunch and sit together.

Luke's Homeroom teacher was Mrs. Patel who greeted each student with a warm smile and said to choose any seat in the room. When the bell rang and everyone was seated, Mrs. Patel took attendance, spoke for a few minutes about school rules and finally handed each child a schedule of classes. Eight minutes later, the bell rang again and Luke was off to his first period class, English.

Luke knew before school started what his schedule would be like, having downloaded the app on his cell phone. He was already looking forward to lunch and seeing LJ and his other friends.

Since seat assignments were alphabetical, Luke wound up in the first row, next to Emily June Butler. Emily was about Luke's height, with gigantic brown eyes and long brown hair. Their English teacher, Mr. Reynolds, took attendance and then asked the students to pair up with the person seated to their right and to spend 5 minutes interviewing each other as a way of breaking the ice in this new environment.

As Luke turned his desk to face Emily, he started to sweat…and sweat….and sweat. Emily asked him if he was okay, to which Luke meekly replied, "Yes, no, maybe, yes, I am." Emily just giggled as Luke tried to wipe the sweat off his forehead with his sleeve. "What's going on with me?" Luke asked himself, a question he would become very familiar with for many years to come.

Emmie, as Emily preferred to be called, was originally from Atlanta, took both ballet and singing lessons and was the youngest of three sisters. Her oldest sister was a senior in high school while her middle sister was an eighth grader in the middle school. Her family had been to

Europe twice, owned a rather large fishing boat and told Luke that both of her parents were attorneys.

She told him that she loved dark chocolate but her favorite food was pasta and could eat it every night. She also said she started taking golf lessons over the summer and couldn't wait to play again on the weekend. Luke was overwhelmed. So much so, in fact, that he lost track of time and barely had a minute to tell Emmie about himself. He didn't even think about soccer.

The rest of the morning passed rather quickly as Luke and Emmie went their separate ways. When the bell rang for lunch, Luke caught up with LJ in the cafeteria, sat down at a long table with a few more of their friends and started comparing notes. All Luke could talk about was Emmie and how he couldn't stop sweating.

As he continued with his story, Luke noticed Emmie at a table at the far end of the cafeteria, seated with another girl who looked just like her, only slightly bigger. He also noticed both girls looking over at him, laughing and smiling. "Oh great." Luke kept saying. "Now everyone will call me The Sweater."

The bus ride home was uneventful, although Luke kept thinking that either anytime someone looked at him or laughed, it was because they had heard about the sweating. Walking into his house and facing a barrage of questions from his mom, Luke just wanted to go to his room, bury his face in the pillow and forget the whole day. "I'll be down in 10 minutes," he told his mom who kissed him on the cheek.

As he climbed the steps to his room, Luke turned to his her and said, "This wasn't what I expected," and disappeared into the bathroom. His mom, left speechless, only wondered what he meant.

Ten minutes turned into an hour. Luke's mom finally called and said it was time to come down. Luke's dad had just arrived home and both parents were concerned. Luke just wondered what he was going to say.

After the usual questions were asked, the ones about subjects and teachers, and answered with one-word answers, Luke fell silent. His mom and dad had never seen him this way but they tried to ignore it. Finally, as the dishes were being cleared, Luke spoke. "I guess you're wondering why I'm so quiet," he said. "Something happened today at the beginning of school and I'm a little upset."

He proceeded to tell them about Emmie and his sweating, ending the story with the fear of being teased at school and being called the Sweater.

His parents, greatly relieved, stared down at the table, trying to keep their smiles hidden from Luke. Finally, his dad spoke. "Luke, did I ever tell how your mom and I met? We were both at the ice skating rink with our own friends. I wasn't a very good skater and accidentally skated into your mom, knocking her to the ice. Before I could even say 'I'm sorry' and, as I extended my hand to help her up, the sweat started pouring down my arm. There was so much sweat that your mom just laughed, got up on her own and skated away. I later found out, after we had been dating for a few months, that her friends had given me the nickname of the Sweater."

Luke's mom smiled, got up from her chair and gave both Luke and his dad a kiss on the cheek. Luke asked to be excused, went to his room, laid down on his bed and just wondered about his dad's story. As he drifted off into a light sleep, his last thoughts were of Emmie and would this ever happen again….

ABOUT THE AUTHOR

Ted Bross (PapaTed) is a wannabe high school English teacher who enjoys the beach, golf, nice restaurants, coffee after his morning run, soccer and….of course, seeing his children and grandchildren. He played soccer in both high school and college and later coached both his own children and collegiate players. He has a doctorate in Adult Development and Learning that did not help him at all in writing this book.

www.ingramcontent.com/pod-product-compliance
Lightning Source LLC
LaVergne TN
LVHW011900060526
838200LV00054B/4446